BABY-SITTERS LITTLE SISTER®

KAREN'S SLEEPOVER

DON'T MISS THE OTHER BABY-SITTERS LITTLE SISTER GRAPHIC NOVELS!

KAREN'S WITCH

KAREN'S ROLLER SKATES

KAREN'S WORST DAY

KAREN'S KITTYCAT CLUB

KAREN'S SCHOOL PICTURE

KAREN'S BIRTHDAY

KAREN'S HAIRCUT

ANN M. MARTIN

BABY-SITTERS LITTLE SISTER®

KAREN'S SLEEPOVER

A GRAPHIC NOVEL BY

KATY FARINA

WITH COLOR BY BRADEN LAMB

graphix
An Imprint of
SCHOLASTIC

This book is in honor of the birth of Emma Feiwel
A. M. M.

To all the readers who have joined me on
my adventures with Karen
K. F.

Library of Congress Control Number: 2023943590

ISBN 978-93-5471-973-8

Printed in India at Sterling Graphics PVT. LTD., Manesar

First edition, May 2024

This Reprint Edition, March 2025

Edited by Cassandra Pelham Fulton
Creative Director: Phil Falco
Publisher: David Saylor

CHAPTER 1

Grrrrr!
Help! Help me!
I'm lost!
And a bear is after me!
Frolic
I'll save you!
Hey, bear! Go away. Shoo!

You can't say "shoo" to a bear!
You say "shoo" to a fly, or maybe even a cat or a small dog.
Oh yeah. What do you say to a bear?
I'm not sure.
My name is Karen Brewer. I am seven years old.
Nancy
Hannie
Today, I am playing Going Camping with my best friends, Hannie Papadakis and Nancy Dawes.

Well, I'm tired.
I think it's bedtime.
We need to set up our sleeping bags first.

I wish we had real sleeping bags out here.
That would be so, so cool.
I have a real sleeping bag, but it's at my house.
We have real sleeping bags, too, but they're in our attic.
The last time we used them was when Kristy had a sleepover.

Sleepovers sound like fun. I have never, ever been to one.
Me neither.
I bet you get to do all sorts of great things at a sleepover.
The sleeping bag part would be really fun.
Yeah.
Do you think we're too young to go to a sleepover?
Of course not! Seven is old enough to do anything.

You can't drive when you're seven.
Nooooo...
But you could have a sleepover...
And I'm going to have one!
You are?!
Yes. Yes, I am.
I will have one right here at Daddy's house. If Daddy and Elizabeth say I can.

Daddy's house is perfect for a sleepover party.
It is a very big and exciting house.
Mommy's house is smaller
and much more quiet.
Wow!

Mommy and Daddy live in different houses because they
are divorced and are now married to different people.
Daddy married Elizabeth, and Mommy married Seth.
Daddy
Elizabeth
Mommy
Seth
Rocky
Shannon
Midgie
Boo-Boo
My brother, Andrew, and I spend most of our time
at Mommy's house, but we live at Daddy's every other
weekend and for two weeks during the summer.

Since Andrew and I live at two houses, I call us the two-twos. We have two of almost everything.
Clothes
Birthdays
7
Toys

Being a two-two is mostly fun, but it is not always easy.
For example, I used to have only one special blanket -- Tickly.

I kept forgetting Tickly at one house or the other, so I decided to rip him in half. That way, I could have one half at each house.
Ouch...
RIIIIIP!

I like the little house when I want peace and quiet. It's much easier to do my homework at the little house.
Plus my pet, Emily Junior, lives there. I love playing with her.

Here is why the big house is perfect for my sleepover:
My little sister!
Bonus Grandma!
Emily Michelle, 2
Nannie
(Elizabeth's mom)
Sam, 14
Tease
David Michael, 7
Charlie, 16
He can drive!
Four older step-siblings!
SO MUCH ROOM!
Kristy, 13
(Coolest big sister EVER!)
BSC
The two houses are very different, and I am lucky to have both.

Bye, you guys! I'll see you on Monday!
Hannie lives across the street from Daddy's and can walk home.
Nancy lives across the street from Mommy's house! I have one best friend at each house.
Sometimes I wish Mommy and Daddy were still married to each other, but being a two-two isn't bad at all.
SKIP!

Daddy? Elizabeth? Um, I have something to ask you.
What is it?
Can I have a sleepover party for my friends? And can I please have it here?
Daddy and Elizabeth are talking with their eyes. I can always tell.

I don't see why not.
All **right!** Thank you, Daddy! Thank you, Elizabeth!
I can't wait to tell my friends. Monday can't come soon enough!

CHAPTER 2
Guess what! Guess what!
Indoor voice, please, Karen.
Oops. Sorry, Ms. Colman.
???
ZOOM!
Hannie! Nancy!
PAT!

What?
Daddy told me I could have a sleepover party!
Whisper...
You're kidding!
Really?
NOD
NOD
What's the secret?
I'm having a sleepover party...

And, Natalie, **you're** invited!
Thanks!
I'm having a sleepover party...and **you're** invited!
Oh puh-**lease** can I come to your sleepover? I'll bring my best pajamas, and --
This sleepover is just for girls.

All girls?
All the girls in our class.
Well, I'm gonna come, too. I am going to crash your party.
No, you're not.
I would not have minded if Ricky Torres came. We like each other.
But this sleepover is for girls only. No boys allowed!

Then I'm going to come spy on your party. And I'll wait until you're least expecting it...
And scare all you girls!
CLOUDY
Eee! Nooo!
What party?
Chatter
Chatter
Chatter

September
September
I have been thinking about my sleepover party for two whole weeks.
I already told all the girls in my class, but should I make **official** invitations? And what do you do at a sleepover? I don't know. I am stuck.
scratch scratch
Party List
But I know just who to ask for help!
Kristy and her friends in The Baby-sitters Club have lots of sleepovers. She is an expert.

Kristy?
Yeah?
Are you very busy?
Not too busy. What's up?
Do you need help with something?
My sleepover party.
What do I need to buy?
Party List
Mostly food.
What kind of food?
Party List
Let's make that list.

Pizza is good for dinner because you can get different toppings and let people pick their favorite.
Then for snacks, you can get popcorn, chips, pretzels...
Do we need any party decorations?
Nope.
We don't?!

Maybe a few.
Now, what do you **do** at a sleepover?
Well, you don't sleep much. You do lots of other things. You watch a spooky movie and scare yourselves.
You make a batch of fudge --
Can we make chocolate chip cookies?

Sure. Then you gossip. You raid the refrigerator. And you stay up as late as you can.
My friends and I always play Truth or Dare and try on makeup, but I think you guys are too young for that.
We are not!
To be honest, I don't think we will get to those things, anyway. This list is big enough.
Boy, we'll have an awful lot to do at the party.
Thank you, Kristy!
You're welcome.

Daddy, can you help me write my invitations?
Come to a sleepover!
Bring your sleeping bag!
(Let me know if you don't have one)
We will watch a movie.
We will eat pizza.
We will make cookies.
Maybe we will try on makeup.
SPARKLE HORSE

David Michael, Andrew, you have to stay away from my sleepover party. No boys allowed.

You too! No boys allowed at my party.
CHIP
Okay, goofball.
CHIP
Charlie, do you mind telling us a ghost story? As long as you leave when it's finished.
Sure thing, kiddo!
Ruffle Ruffle
Oh, boy! This is going to be the best sleepover **ever**!

CHAPTER 3
Thank you for the invitation, Karen. I like the stickers you used.
Yeah, thanks!
You're welcome.
Didn't you send **me** an invitation?
Of course I did. I mailed it with the other invitations. I mailed them all at the same time.

I bet yours got lost in the mail. Give it a couple more days.
Anyway, you know you're invited to the party whether you get an invitation or not.
But I **want** an invitation.
I'm sure it will be waiting for you when we get home from school today.
But it wasn't.

It wasn't there on Thursday, either.
Nancy didn't talk to me at all on the way to school Friday morning.
I guess Karen did not invite me after all. I guess she never mailed me an invitation. She doesn't want me at her sleepover.
And I even have my own sleeping bag. I wouldn't need to borrow one.

I do too want you at my party!
You don't mean that. I am the only girl in the class who did not get an invite.
NING
SNOW
But I **sent** you one!
Time to take your seats, class.

scribble
scribble
scribble
scribble
Yes, Nancy?
Karen is drawing in her book.

Have you finished your work, Karen?
No...
Are you having trouble with the work?
No.
You know you are not supposed to draw in books, don't you?
Yes.
Then you will have to stay inside during recess today. You will erase your drawings and think about what you did.
Ms. Colman has never punished me before.

And Nancy.
Yes?
No more tattling, please.
Okay. I'm sorry.
Boy, Nancy is **really** mad at me.
ENGLISH 2
RIIIINNG
erase erase
CLOUDY

Hardly anyone ever has to miss recess.
Erase
Erase
Erase
And I'm sure Ms. Colman is angry with me, even though she doesn't look angry.
I **do** know you're not supposed to draw in books. Only in coloring books or a sketchbook.
But I never would have tattled on Nancy if **she** were drawing in **her** book.
What am I supposed to do?

BRRRIIING!!
Thankfully, Nancy and I do not have to ride home together.
We didn't talk to each other for most of the day.
I feel really, really terrible.

Sigh...
Karen, you have a phone call.
Hopefully it's Kristy. Talking to her might make me feel better.
?

Hello?
Hi!
Who is this, please?
It's me, silly. It's Nancy!
Why is Nancy calling?
Yeah?
Guess what?

It came! It came! The invitation to your sleepover came this afternoon!
Good.
Karen, I'm sorry I got you in trouble today. Honest. I was just mad about the invitation. I promise I'll never tell on you again.
...
Okay? I'm **really** sorry.
But thank you, thank you, **thank you** for inviting me!
So...what can I bring to the party?

Nothing.
You're not invited after all. I un-invite you.
People who get me in trouble with Ms. Colman do **not** come to my sleepovers.
SLAM!
SMACK!

PACE PACE PACE PACE PACE
Part of me feels pleased.
I made Nancy feel as bad as I feel.
The other part of me feels awful.
I don't like feeling bad, so Nancy must not like feeling bad, either.
And I was the one who made her feel that way.
I don't know what to think.
Nancy is my best friend.
How mad can best friends get?

What if we never, ever speak to each other again?
I almost want to call her back.
I would tell Nancy:
"I'm sorry I un-invited you. Now you are re-invited. You can come after all!"

But I just can't.
Nancy got me in trouble at school.
And a best friend is not supposed to do that.

CHAPTER 4

Karen, sometimes best friends fight, but that does not mean they will never be friends again.

Mommy is worried because Nancy said that she would never ride in the same car with me again.
I guess.
And sometimes when best friends fight, they hurt each other's feelings.
You and Nancy don't want to do that, do you?
We already have.
Nancy and I are not friends anymore. We are best enemies.

STONEYBROOK ACADEMY
STONEYBROOK ACADEMY
I can't wait until Saturday!
Me neither!

I'm going to borrow my sister's sleeping bag. I don't have one of my own yet.
Me too.
I am so excited for the party! But I can't sleep over. We already have plans for that night.
That's okay, Sara. I'm glad you can still come over for a little bit!
Karen, are your brothers going to be at the party?
They might be at home, but they are **not** coming to the party.

What if they play tricks on us?
What if they give us spicy chewing gum or hide a rubber snake in someone's sleeping bag?
Augh! A rubber snake!
They will not play tricks. I will not let them.
I might play tricks.
You!
You are not coming to my party. It's just for us girls.

Yes, I am coming.
And I'm going to throw pebbles at your windows and scare you.
Nooo!
And I'll bring a handful of rubber snakes.
No!
And then I'll hide them in all your sleeping bags!
HA HA HA HA
You are not going to do those things, Ricky, and you know it.

Hee Hee
HA HA
HA HA
Hee Hee
HA HA
I feel pretty sorry for Nancy.
It is not fun to be left out of anything.
HA HA
HA HA
It makes you feel gigundo bad.
But how can I ask my best enemy
to come to my sleepover?
hmph

STONEYBROOK ACADEMY
On Wednesday morning, something different happened.
Class, I have a surprise.
Today, a new student is going to join our class. I hope you will make her feel --
CREAK

Swing
step
step
step
Class, this is Pamela Harding.
Pamela, maybe you can tell us a little about yourself.

My name is Pamela Harding. My family just moved to Stoneybrook.
My mother writes books and my father is a dentist. I have a sixteen-year-old sister. She lets me wear her perfume.
TOSS
WHOA!
She looks so cool!
Pamela, you may sit at my desk until a custodian brings in your own.
Lucky duck! No one has sat at Ms. Colman's desk before.

We really want Pamela to be our friend!
EXIT

I'm having a sleepover this Saturday, Pamela.
Most of the girls in our class are coming. Can you come, too?
Sure. I guess so.
Shrug
See? She did not need an invitation in the mail.
Pamela is very, very cool.

CHAPTER 5
Saturday has come at last!
Woo-hoo!
ZOOM!

Let's go shopping for the sleepover! We have to buy all the things on the list.
We cannot forget the balloons. And we have to order pizza!
Whoa, calm down.
Please sit down and have breakfast first.
Plop!
Fidget
Fidget
Fidget
What if the stores run out of popcorn or balloons or something?!

I don't think that will happen.
Karen, would you like me to take you shopping after breakfast?
Yeah!
MUNCH MUNCH MUNCH
pie pops
BRAN
GRAIN CLUMP
CLOWN HOOPS
sugar stripe
Grape GRITS!
K IS FOR CORN!
RICE ELF
Hmmm...
CHIP
CHIPZ
RAISIN

SODA!!!
Kristy! Kristy!
What is it?
Will you help me get ready for my party?
Sure.

MY DONKEY PRINCESS
BASKETOONS
FIRE HERO
The playroom looks so, so pretty now that it is all decorated.
Thank you, Kristy.
You're welcome.

I should remind everyone else how to behave today.
I do not want my family to embarrass me, especially in front of Pamela.
David Michael, you better leave me and my friends alone.
Don't worry. I do not want to hang out with you girls.
Sam, Charlie, you leave us alone, too.

Maybe I will, maybe I won't.
I will stay out of your way except for the ghost story.
Thank you.
Andrew, please do not get shy or act like a baby.
Emily, please do not dribble food out of your mouth.
DING-DONG!

I bet the first one here is Hannie since she lives right across the street.
Oh!
Hi, Pamela. Come on in. You look really nice.
Thank you.
Were we supposed to get dressed up?

I feel underdressed compared to how cool Pamela looks.
Oh, you didn't bring a sleeping bag. That's all right. You can use one of ours.
I won't need one.
I would **never** sleep on the floor. I **have** to sleep in a bed.
Oh, um. I guess you can use my bed tonight.
Hmph!

Uh-oh. What if all my friends want to sleep in beds?
DING-DONG!
Goody!
Jannie, Hannie, Natalie, and Sara are here! Sara's dad is going to stay until it's time for them to leave.
Come in, you guys!

Okay! Let's go up to the playroom.
To the playroom? You have a playroom?
Yes, we have a playroom. I have a little brother and sister.
Now I **really** wish Nancy were here.
She usually knows what to say.

Twirl
Twirl
Look what I brought!
It's really for playing dress-up.
Hee Hee
Hee Hee Hee
I brought -- ta-da!
My musical puppy!
Look. You push this button and he moves his head.
CLICK!

How much is that ♫ ♪ ♫ doggie in the window
He's sooo cute!
SPRAY! SPRAY! SPRAY!
Augghhh!
Gotcha!
David Michael!
Nyeh-heh-heh

Ha ha ha
Ha ha
Eww, gross!
Bleh.
Ha ha
Hee hee hee
I think most of my friends didn't mind David Michael's surprise attack.
But is my sleepover party off to a good start or a bad start? I just don't know.

CHAPTER 6
Who's hungry?
I am!
What's for dinner?
Pizza.
Yay!
Pizza gives me bad breath. I can't eat it.
Oh. Maybe Elizabeth or Kristy can fix you something else.

Um, Natalie, Leslie, Hannie, will you help me carry everything?
We can eat in here but we have to be careful not to spill.
Okay!
Hey...

Do you think Pamela is having any fun?
I think Pamela is... well, I don't think she is any fun.
She makes me feel like a baby.
Here we are!
My big sister made you a peanut butter and jelly sandwich.

It only has a little peanut butter, in case you're afraid it will stick to the roof of your mouth or give you peanut butter breath.
snort
hee hee
I think most of the girls still want Pamela to like them.
But I bet Nancy wouldn't care. I wish she were here.
PIZZA
Okay, time for a spooky movie. Guess what I chose to watch with dinner?
What?

The Wizard of Oz!
Oh, goody! The witch is so scary.
So are the flying monkeys.
That is a baby movie.
It is not!

Toto, I have a feeling we're not in Kansas anymore...
There's no place like home...
There's no place like home...
sigh
Phew! I didn't think she was going to make it.
Haven't you ever seen the movie before?
Scoff

No. Have you?
Only about eighty-seven times. We own the movie.
Well, so do we, but it still scares me.
Boy, do I miss Nancy. If you think I have a big mouth, you should hear her.
CLICK!

Who wants to make cookies?
What kind?
Chocolate chip.
Hooray! That's my favorite!
Kristy, can you help us bake some cookies?

Sure thing.
How come your sister is baby-sitting you?
She is not baby-sitting. She is just helping.

PIZZA
FLOUR
Fwuump!
POOF!
SPLAT!

HA HA! HEE HEE HEE!
HA HA HA!
TOSS
THROW
Look what I made!

Who does this look like?
Ricky Torres!
Yeah!
Hee Hee Hee
Hee Hee
Okay, let's really make the cookies now.
Sweep
Sweep

Who wants to eat Ricky?
I just can't.
I'll eat him.
Ka-runch!
Augh! That hurt!

Hee hee
Hee hee
munch munch
...
Sara, it's time to head home.
Aww, already?
Aww!

Bye, Karen! Thank you for inviting me to your party.
Bye, Sara! Thank you so much for coming.
yawwwn
Karen, wait a moment.
Are you having a good time?
No.

Pamela Harding is ruining everything. I don't know what to do.
I really, **really** wish Nancy were here.

CHAPTER 7
Where is Nancy?
Did she get sick or something?
No. We had a fight.
About what?
Nancy didn't get her invitation in the mail when everyone else did. She thought I had not invited her to my party.

She was mad and she tattled on me and got me in trouble with Ms. Colman.
Then Nancy got her invitation.
She called and said she wasn't mad anymore. But I was mad, so I un-invited her.
We have not spoken to each other for a whole week.
Wow. That's a big fight. I bet you wish it were over now, don't you?

Do I ever! I really need Nancy here. She would know what to do about Pamela.
But what I really want is to make up with Nancy.
I don't know how to do that, though. And I feel funny inviting her to my party **now**.
I think you should call her.
Apologize to her. She already apologized to you. And say you forgive her for getting you in trouble.

She was just angry then, Karen. People do all sorts of things when they are angry.
And I bet Nancy would rather come to your party late than not at all.
I don't know. Maybe...
Call her. It is the mature thing to do.
Well. I am a very mature person for a seven-year-old.
Okay. I'll call her.

Riiiiing-CLICK!
Hello, Mrs. Dawes speaking.
Hi. This is Karen. Is Nancy there?
Sure. Hold on a sec.
Hello?
Nancy, I'm **really** sorry I un-invited you to my party. I did that because you made me feel bad when you got me in trouble. I know you feel bad now, though.

So I think our fight should be over.
And I want you to come to my party right away.
You do? Thanks!
And, Karen, I am sorry I got you in trouble.
That was a mean thing to do. Do you forgive me?
Fidget
Fidget
Oh, yes! I forgive you.
Do you forgive me?
Yes, I do.

Good. Then come over right away. You won't believe Pamela.
She is making us all feel like babies.
She is? How?
She thought **The Wizard of Oz** was not a scary movie, when everyone knows it is.
I mean, duh.
And she will not sleep in a sleeping bag. And she wouldn't have pizza with us because she said it gives her bad breath.
Now she is just sitting while everyone else makes cookies.

She looks like she thinks we are jerks. Maybe even dweebs.
She is ruining everything.
Please come to my sleepover. I really need you!

RUUUmmble
Knock
Knock
Hey, how come you brought two sleeping bags?
Yeah, how come?

I heard that Pamela doesn't have a sleeping bag, so I brought one for her.
I sleep in **beds.**
How boring.
Boy, what a storm! It is so, so scary out there.
My father said we're really in for it.

What's that supposed to mean?
It means we are in great danger.
Maybe this is a good time for Charlie to tell us a ghost story. He promised he would.
Ooh, I don't know...

Oh, it will only be fun-scary. Promise.
This is the story of a ghost who haunts a big mansion.
The people who live there only see him when it rains.

The ghost wears a bucket on his head, so people call him Buckethead.
But he hates that name.
Every night that it rains, Buckethead wanders the halls, saying, "I will get you! I will get revenge!"
flop
scoot
scoot
YOINK!
AAHHHHHHH!

Then, on one really rainy night, the people in the house heard clanking sounds.
Like chains being rattled.
A girl saw a white figure standing at the end of her bed.
CRASH!
The figure howled, "Soooooon, I will take my reveeeeenge!"
KA-BOOM!
AHHHHHH!

CHAPTER 8

Sob
Sob
Sob
Help! Oh, help!
Where am I?
I can't see a thing!
I'm scared!
Sob
Sob
Calm down, you guys! We probably just blew a fuse or something. I'll go check the fuse box.
Nooo! Don't leave us!
How about if I send Kristy up here to stay with you?
That's fine. Thank you, Charlie.
Sob Sob Sob

Sniff
sniffle
snort
STEP
STEP
STEP...
STEP
STEP
STEP
Eee! It's Buckethead!
Who's Buckethead?
It's just my sister.
Don't worry.

DONKEY PRINCESS
BASKETOONS
Did Charlie look at the fuse box?
He didn't need to. And I'm afraid I have a little bit of bad news.
Oh no!
What kind of bad news?
It's not a problem with our fuse box. There's a blackout.
We looked outside and there are no lights on anywhere.
That means nobody in our neighborhood has any power.

I want to go home!
Wimp.
Sob sob sob
My big brother told me that thunder is really just giants bowling. He said that if a ball rolls into the gutter, it will fall out of the sky.
It could crash right through the roof of your house!
My brother says that lightning is caused by angry ghosts. And if they're angry enough, they will send a lightning bolt right down to the ground.
CRASH!

It's okay, you guys. Haven't you heard about cold fronts and warm fronts?
Sob Sob Sob
Sob Sob
No, what's that?
A thunderstorm is just weather. That's all.
When air is unstable, like if it rises up instead of staying still, and the air is wet, then you get a thunderstorm.
sniff sniff
See, the big, dark thunderclouds are charged with electricity...

Do you know what she's talking about?
No.
BLINK!
Hooray!

Do you guys know enough about thunderstorms now?
Yes.
Because I can teach you some more things --
NO!
Hee hee hee!
Ahem!

Girls?
Yes?
Bedtime now, okay? You've had plenty of excitement for one night.
All right. We'll get ready for bed now. Good night, Daddy.
Sleep tight, girls.
Aww, Karen, we have to go to bed now?
But Karen, it's so **early**!
I only go to bed this early on **school** nights.

We're not **really** going to bed now.
We are just going to pretend.
We'll put on our pajamas and get into our sleeping bags --
Or beds.
Whatever. Anyway, then we will talk and tell stories until midnight.
Then we are going to do something special. But first we have to wait for Daddy and Elizabeth and everyone else to go to sleep.
What is it?
Secret.

Now, come on. Let's get ready for bed before Daddy comes back and has to tell us a second time.
BASKETOONS
BASKETOONS
Are you sure you don't want to borrow my extra sleeping bag? I brought it just for you.
I am very sure.

Come on, Pamela. I'll show you where my room is.
I hope you like my bed.
...
What are those?
They are Tickly and Moosie.
Baby things?

No!
SNATCH
Do you still sleep with them?
See you at midnight.
Suddenly I am very glad that Pamela is not sleeping with us in the playroom.
My **friends** would **never** make fun of Tickly or Moosie.

CHAPTER 9

SSHHHHAA
I have a question.
Who here likes Pamela?
. . .
I like her. She is cool. She's so grown-up.

I wish my mother would let me wear clothes like Pamela's.
Me too.
Thinking she is grown-up and liking her clothes isn't the same as liking Pamela.
I think Pamela is a jerk.
gasp
I don't want to talk about Pamela anymore.
What is the scariest thing that has happened to anyone here?

Getting lost at Disney World.
Something like that happened to me, too!
I had a friend named Betsy who used to come over all the time, but Mommy and Daddy don't remember her.
Was she a ghost?!
Hee Hee Hee
Ha ha ha

Ha ha ha ha!
Hey, you guys! It's almost midnight!
You better go get Pamela.

I'll let her get her beauty rest.
Pamela is sleeping, so we will have to go without her.
"Go"?
Yeah! Guess what? It's time to...
raid the refrigerator!
YAY!
SHHH!
We have to be very quiet, and we can't turn on any lights.

NO SNAK

Help yourselves!
1% MILK
grrroowwl...
Wait, what was that?

AAAHHHH!!
HA HA HA HA HA HA HA!
Sam!
HA HA HA HA HA!
What's going on here?
Everybody back to bed. And I mean it.

Good night, everyone.
Sorry we couldn't raid the fridge.
That's okay. Good night, Karen.
ZZZZZZ...

blink
blink blink
blink
Morning!
Morning! Guess what time it is.
Seven thirty?
Nope. Ten o'clock.
Ten o'clock!

Everybody, get up. It's breakfast time. It's almost lunchtime!
Pamela, time to get up!
Knock Knock
Where are your blankie and stuffie?
Never mind.

Well, here are the sleepyheads.
How about a picnic breakfast in the yard?
Okay! Thanks, Daddy.

Karen! Jannie's mother is here!
Aww. Bye, everyone.
Bye, Jannie.

I hope Pamela's parents come next.
munch munch
HONK HONK!
That is my mommy's car.
I am not sad to see Pamela go. She has been gigundo mean about Moosie, Tickly, and lots of other things.
I've decided that I do not want to be Pamela's friend.
munch munch

Bye, Pamela. Thanks for coming.
See you in school!

Phew!

CHAPTER 10
Wave Wave
Wave Wave
Haha!
I'm glad I get to stay over until your mommy takes you back to the little house.
I'm glad you guys aren't fighting anymore.

Me too.
Remember when you and Hannie were mad at each other?
Yup. Remember when you and Hannie were mad at each other?
Yup.
Boy, we should stop fighting. We are lucky that we are friends.
If we were not friends, we might have to be friends with Pamela.

BLECH!
You know what? We are like the Three Musketeers.
Hey! I've got a great idea!
Shuffle Shuffle
TA-DA!
EMBROIDERY THREAD

Let's each pick a color and make friendship bracelets.
That way, the Three Musketeers are always together.
Yeah!

We just need one more thing to make it official.
We are the Three Musketeers
We vow to be friends for life
signed,
Karen Brewer
Nancy Dawes
Hannie Papadakis

Look at my new outfit!
Pamela? Maybe you could come over to my house after school someday.
I want you to come ice skating with me.

Don't Jannie and Sara remember how awful Pamela was at the sleepover?
I guess not.
But I don't care. If those girls want to be friends with Pamela, then let them.
Yeah. We have each other. We're the Three Musketeers now!

Oh yeah! That reminds me. I have your copies of the pact. Mommy made them for us.
We are the Three Musketeers. We vow to be friends for life.

Maybe we should add something to our pact. Something like "And we vow to never be friends with Pamela."
I like our pact the way it is.
Who cares about Pamela, anyway?
They do.

The girls like Pamela's glamour. But they don't know the real Pamela that is underneath.
Will they find out? And if they do, will they still like her? Will they care?
Well, I know one thing for certain.
Even if Pamela becomes Queen of the Classroom, the Three Musketeers will stick together.
Right.
Through thick and thin.
Forever and ever.

What about a secret handshake?
Yeah!
CLAP!
CLAP!
SNAP!!
Hee hee hee
Hee hee
Hee hee hee
Hey, guys!

You know what, Karen? Your sleepover was the best ever.
Even though I have never been to one before.
Hey. I hear your sleepover was really fun. Can I come to the next one?
We'll see.

ANN M. MARTIN'S The Baby-sitters Club is one of the most popular series in the history of publishing — with more than 190 million books in print worldwide — and inspired a generation of young readers. Her novels include *Belle Teal, A Corner of the Universe* (a Newbery Honor book), *Here Today, A Dog's Life,* and *On Christmas Eve,* as well as the much-loved collaborations, *P.S. Longer Letter Later* and *Snail Mail No More,* with Paula Danziger, and *The Doll People* and *The Meanest Doll in the World,* written with Laura Godwin and illustrated by Brian Selznick. Ann lives in upstate New York.

KATY FARINA is the creator of eight *New York Times* bestselling graphic novel adaptations of the Baby-sitters Little Sister series by Ann M. Martin, and of an original graphic novel for young readers, *Song of the Court*. Previously, she painted backgrounds for *She-Ra and the Princesses of Power* at DreamWorks TV. Katy lives in Los Angeles with her husband and two rambunctious cats. Visit her online at katyfarina.com.

DON'T MISS THE OTHER BABY-SITTERS LITTLE SISTER GRAPHIC NOVELS!